I0845186

EXIN Agile Scrum Foundation Exam Practice Questions and Dumps

Exam Prep Tests for Exin

PRESENTED BY
Exam Force Academy

About Exam Force Academy:

Centric Books is an online test accreditation center founded in 2022 by Michael Swartz in San Francisco, CA, USA. We provide resources that allow students and professionals to obtain certifications from various organizations. We have expertise in all areas of Information Technology and Cyber Security with hundreds of Global Clinical, Security, Business Management, and System Management certification providers, so we ensure that our material replicates real-world exam situations and is highly accurate - enabling students and industry officials to easily obtain the their upcoming certifications

QUESTION 1

A customer wants a report that sum up functionality involved and failings noticed and handled, right in the last part of a Sprint. Who might preeminent make this report?

A. The Product Owner
B. The Scrum Master
C. The group
D. This sort of report needs to not be ready.

QUESTION 2

Who needs to upgrade the work estimates in the course of the Sprint?

A. The Development Group
B. The Project Supervisor
C. The Product Owner

QUESTION 3

Which means of communication is the most improved to clarify the elucidation of a necessity?

A. E-mail
B. Face-to-face
C. Instant messaging
D. Telephone

QUESTION 4

In a Scrum project, when will a situation get involved to the Product backlog?

A. When it is progressive, but cannot despite that be free.
B. When the group works on it for a particular release.
C. When the customer wants a new necessity.

QUESTION 5

What is the purpose of the Scrum-of-Scrums meeting?

A. To notify management regarding the progress of the project.
B. Bring together all group members of all groups.
C. Manage the work of many Scrum groups.
D. Kick-off a worldwide Scrum project.

QUESTION 6

In the course of a Sprint, the group bring to an end four stories with story points 3, 5, 8 and 2 in that sequence. They additionally finalize half a story with a story point of 13. What is the velocity of the group?
A. 18
B. 24.5
C. 31

QUESTION 7

Which report defines Release Planning?

A. After viewing at all the stories in the backlog, the group estimates their effort in detail.
B. The group meets with the customer to discuss the scope, cost and time of the release.
C. The group and the Product Owner come to an agreement on an initial plan for the delivery of attributes.

QUESTION 8

Agile planning takes place at many levels as well as a daily plan, a sprint plan and a strategic plan.

What term preeminent states the multi-level planning?

A. Planning Onion
B. Planning Poker
C. Sprint Planning

QUESTION 9

In the course of the release planning meeting, it is tough to agree on priorities.

Sales want to apply several new attributes to become equal with the competitors.

Marketing want to work on a mobile interface that can demonstrate to be a competitive differentiator. Customer support want better logging and auditing capabilities to increase maintainability.

What needs to be done to set the priorities?

A. Approach Senior Management and ask for priorities.
B. Survey the existing customers and prioritize according to their views.
C. The Product Owner will set the priorities.

QUESTION 10

How needs to 'done' be defined when many groups are operating on a
single product?

A. All groups need to have the equivalent meaning of 'done'.
B. Each group wants to define and use their individual meaning of 'done'.
C. The Scrum Master explains when the item is 'done'.

QUESTION 11

Approaching the end of a Sprint, the group recognizes that they will not be
capable to conclude the stories they had dedicated to. What is the
preeminent strategy for the group?
A. Add resources and group members to meet the goals of the present
    Sprint.
B. Ask the Product Owner to Select which stories can be delayed until the
    next Sprint.
C. Agree on a new definition of 'done' for the Sprint Backlog Items.

QUESTION 12

What is an "escaped defect"?

A. A flaw that was noticed by the customer.
B. A flaw that was planned to be handled, but not handled in a Sprint.
C. A flaw the Continuous Integration System failed to catch.

QUESTION 13

When does a Sprint come to an end?

A. When all of the Product Backlog items are done.
B. When all the tasks in the Sprint Backlog are finished.
C. When the Sprint defined time box ends.

QUESTION 14

What message can you give to a customer regarding a main advantage of using Scrum?

A. Scrum will give customers more control over routine activities.
B. Scrum will help the group accept variations into the project at no extra cost.
C. The group will show a presentation of working software each few weeks.

QUESTION 15

A Supervisor wants to go to the daily stand-up meeting so that he can be more quick to respond to the group by being mindful of the group's progress and problems. As the Scrum Master, what needs to you do?

A. Let the Product Owner to take part in 'listen only' mode.
B. Let the Product Owner to take part like any other group member.
C. Turn down the request as the daily stand-up is only for the group.

QUESTION 16

What is the normal length of the time box for the finish Sprint Planning meeting?

A. Four hours for a 30-day Sprint, one to two hours for a shorter Sprint.
B. However long it takes to finalize the Sprint Backlog.
C. Never beyond two hours, irrespective of Sprint length.

QUESTION 17

What is time-boxing?

A. A period of intense activity within a certain release.
B. Setting an upper time limit and planning the activities within that limit.
C. Tight planning focused on reducing the time needed for any activity.

QUESTION 18

What is a feature of a well-designed Agile work space?

A. It has a silent zone to facilitate concentration.
B. There is enough space for information radiators.
C. Work stations are personalized for group members.

QUESTION 19

A big product group attributes six different groups having ten members
each, working on a project that involves four high level attributes. How many
Product Backlogs needs to the group have?
A. 1
B. 4
C. 6

QUESTION 20

What is an information radiator?

A. A physical display for the group that provides information regarding the
present status.
B. A tool that automatically conducts relevant information to the Product
Owner.
C. A status information or dashboard that is maintained by the Scrum
Master.

QUESTION 21

A Scrum group failed to meet the Sprint objectives. One of the main members of the group fell ill and was away for two days right at the start of the four-week Sprint.

What is the most probable cause that the group did not meet the Sprint objectives?

A. The Product Owner is unable to prioritize.
B. The group is lacking skills.
C. The group did not plan the Sprint well.
D. The group is over-worked.

QUESTION 22

A user story was estimated at five ideal hours. On a normal eight hour working day, the group gets approximately four hours of actual work time. What will be the elapsed time needed to bring to an end to the Story?
A. One day and two hours
B. Two days
C. Five hours

QUESTION 23

Who knows most regarding the progress towards a business objective or a release?

A. The Product Owner
B. The Scrum Master
C. The group

QUESTION 24

What is the preeminent way to part groups on a big project which is applied using Scrum?

A. Group by domain expertise.
B. Group by attributes being progressive,
C. Group by specialty of the group members.

QUESTION 25

Collaboration is the most significant parameter for the success of an Agile group. What term preeminent describes this kind of interaction?

A. Distributed group working.
B. Information radiator sharing.
C. Osmotic communication.

QUESTION 26

Why is planning poker an operative estimation technique?

A. It makes a lot of useful discussion and gets group buy-in.
B. It effects in lower estimates as group members will estimate individually.
C. It triggers a more detailed and task-oriented break-up of the story.

QUESTION 27

A group settled to install a big traffic light in the group hall to specify whether the newest build was healthy (green), failing a few tests (orange) or failing high priority tests (red).

What term can be used to define the traffic light?

A. Information radiator
B. Osmotic communication
C. Triangulation

QUESTION 28

Which is a report of value as termed in the Agile manifesto?

A. We value customer collaboration over reacting to variations.
B. We value project management over individuals and interactions.
C. We value processes and tools over comprehensive documentation.
D. We value reacting to change to satisfy the customer.

QUESTION 29

In the course of a Sprint Planning session, the group debates regarding the work estimates for a certain story.
- The Product Owner estimates five days. The Lead Architect estimates
- two days. The Scrum Master estimates eight days.
- The group member working on it estimates seven days.

What value (in days) needs to be used for planning?

A. 2
B. 5
C. 7
D. 8

QUESTION 30

From which sport is the term "Scrum" and much of the terminology
derived?

A. Kick boxing
B. Polo
C. Rugby
D. Soccer

QUESTION 31

What needs to the Scrum Master advise the group to give their main focus,
though working in a global distributed group?

A. Favor conference calls and video chats in order to save on travel
   budget.
B. Place greater importance on group-building activities and cultural
   sensitivities.
C. Give at least four hours of overlap time by shifting working hours.

QUESTION 32

A group decide on a Product Backlog Item (PBI) for the Sprint Backlog.
What must a group do to finish the Product Backlog Item it selects?
A. As much as can be done in the Sprint before the deadline.
B. As much as is needed to satisfy the definition of 'done'.
C. Analyze, design, program, test and document the PBI.

QUESTION 33

An engineering organization is transforming their project management technique to use Agile Scrum. What is the preeminent approach to the transformation?

A. Get a senior executive to champion the transformation.
B. Get the group supervisors to monitor their group's progress on a daily basis.
C. Make a swift transition and start using Scrum for all projects.

QUESTION 34

Which of the given reports preeminent expresses the role that the daily stand-up meeting plays in the monitoring of a Scrum project?

A. The stand-up meeting helps the Scrum Master to upgrade the burn-down chart.
B. The stand-up meeting provides the group insight into their progress and their problems.
C. The stand-up meeting lets the Product Owner review the progress of the group.

QUESTION 35

What is the relationship amid the Product Backlog, the Release Backlog and the Sprint Backlog?

A. The Product Backlog is a subset of the Sprint Backlog, which is a subset of the Release Backlog.

B. The Release Backlog is a subset of the Product Backlog, which is a subset of the Sprint Backlog

C. The Sprint Backlog is a subset of the Product Backlog, which is a subset of the Release Backlog.

QUESTION 36

What is the expected outcome of the first Sprint on a project?

A. A few working, tested attributes from the Product Backlog
B. Architecture and high-level design of the Product
C. Assignment of the group, Product Owner and Scrum Master
D. A well-defined release plan for the Product

QUESTION 37

Who is the owner of a Sprint Backlog Item in the course of the Sprint
Planning meeting?

A. The entire group owns all Sprint Backlog Items.
B. The Product Owner owns all Sprint Backlog Items.
C. The group member working on the item owns that item.

QUESTION 38

A group is trying to convince a customer regarding the value of adopting
Scrum. The customer likes several of the attributes of the methodology like
the bi-weekly presentation, but the customer remains mainly unconvinced
of the value of Scrum and refuses to change the way of working,

What needs to the group do?

A. Let the Scrum Master 'translate' to Waterfall practices.
B. Use Scrum and convince the customer in the course of the process.
C. Do not follow Scrum until the customer is convinced of the value.

QUESTION 39

The group determines that it has over-dedicated itself for a Sprint. Who needs to be present when reviewing and adjusting the Sprint work?

    A. The group, the Scrum Master and the Product Owner. The Stakeholders needs to be consulted.

    B. The group and the Scrum Master. The Product Owner needs to be consulted.

    C. The group only. The Product Owner needs to be consulted.

QUESTION 40

Why are estimates expressed in terms of story points tough to explain outside of the group?

    A. It requires a comparison to a benchmark, which typically varies from group to group.

    B. It requires a deeper understanding of the technical approach to fulfil each story.

    C. It requires breaking the stories down into Sprint Backlog Items, which only the group can do.

QUESTION 41

You want to convince a customer of the advantages of Scrum. What is the main advantage of Scrum for the customer?

    A. Scrum ensures that the customer receives value early in the project.

    B. Scrum will give customers more control over day-to-day activities.

    C. Scrum will help the Group accept variations into the project at no extra cost.

QUESTION 42

In the course of the Daily Scrum three questions are answered. Which
question is one of these questions?
   A. What has been accomplished since the last meeting?
   B. Who needs to take on the next task?
   C. Which wants of the customer did we receive?

QUESTION 43

A Scrum Group is estimating User Stories. The Scrum Master suggests the
Affinity Estimation technique. What is the process of Affinity Estimation?
   A. Compare the Story to reference Stories and then estimate it.
   B. Estimate on your own, then discuss everyone else's estimates.
   C. Sort all Stories based on their relative effort needed.

QUESTION 44

An often-used preeminent practice is to define User Stories according to
the acronym 'INVEST'. The 'I' of INVEST signifies Independent. Suppose
that you have a User Story that is **not** Independent.

What is the consequence of having dependent User Stories?

   A. You do not have enough knowledge to build the item.
   B. You wants to work on the item together with another Scrum group.
   C. You need more people to build the item.
   D. You will not be able to order them based on their business values.

QUESTION 45

For the Development Group and the Scrum Master, the Daily Scrum is mandatory. Other roles might only take part without speaking. What is the most significant reason that other roles are not permitted to speak?
A. For the reason that it is not a status meeting for all stockholders.
B. For the reason that other people speaking will let the meeting run late.
C. For the reason that the meeting is just for updating the work done.

QUESTION 46

Sprint duration is typically handled at one month or less. Why is that?

A. For the reason that customers cannot wait longer than a month.
B. For the reason that it is tough to focus on the same thing for longer.
C. For the reason that this keeps the complexity and risk acceptable.

QUESTION 47

A Scrum Group works on a project in 2-week Sprints. In the course of the Sprint Planning meeting of the third Sprint, the Product Owner says:
"I will be going on holiday in 2 weeks. Let's change the duration of this Sprint to 4 weeks, so that I will be back when it ends."

Should the duration of the sprint be increased?

A. Yes, for the reason that the Product Owner wants to be available at the end of a Sprint.
B. Yes, for the reason that Sprint duration can be anything amid 2 and 4 weeks.
C. No, for the reason that the Sprint duration is not based on single events.
D. No, for the reason that only Development Group members might change Sprint duration.

QUESTION 48

Which Scrum event is meant to look back and progress upon the finished Sprint?

A. Release Sprint
B. Sprint Retrospective
C. Sprint Review

ANSWER

1. Correct Answer: B
2. Correct Answer: A
3. Correct Answer: B
4. Correct Answer: C
5. Correct Answer: C
6. Correct Answer: A
7. Correct Answer: C
8. Correct Answer: A
9. Correct Answer: C
10. Correct Answer: A
11. Correct Answer: B
12. Correct Answer: A
13. Correct Answer: C
14. Correct Answer: C
15. Correct Answer: A
16. Correct Answer: A
17. Correct Answer: B
18. Correct Answer: B
19. Correct Answer: A
20. Correct Answer: A
21. Correct Answer: C
22. Correct Answer: A
23. Correct Answer: A
24. Correct Answer: B
25. Correct Answer: C
26. Correct Answer: A
27. Correct Answer: A
28. Correct Answer: D
29. Correct Answer: C
30. Correct Answer: C
31. Correct Answer: B
32. Correct Answer: B
33. Correct Answer: A
34. Correct Answer: B
35. Correct Answer: C
36. Correct Answer: A
37. Correct Answer: A
38. Correct Answer: C

39. Correct Answer: C
40. Correct Answer: A
41. Correct Answer: A
42. Correct Answer: A
43. Correct Answer: C
44. Correct Answer: D
45. Correct Answer: A
46. Correct Answer: C
47. Correct Answer: B
48. Correct Answer: B